I have Autism...

What's that?

**By Kate Doherty
Paddy McNally
Eileen Sherrard**

Foreword

Children and adults with autism have life-long difficulties so it is important to expand methods to help those affected.

There are many ways in which this may be offered. For example, where I work at Division TEACCH in the University of North Carolina, our programme works closely with parents to help them understand autism. It gives parents the knowledge and skills to help their special children.

It has developed teaching strategies to help people with autism learn skills in communication, independence, and daily living. Training professionals who work with children or adults with autism is also necessary in any successful programme.

There are additional needs for clients who are in the higher range of ability and also those who have some degree of learning difficulties. These individuals often have 'insight' about their condition and are sometimes considered to be the 'fortunate' ones.

However, this awareness of differences can result in low confidence and other problems for the person with autism.

This booklet has tried to help these individuals in a way that is sensitive and clinically sound. The authors have highlighted problems faced by individuals with autism and addressed these clearly and simply.

The topics are those that directly affect the lives of people with autism. The explanation of 'differences' between people with autism and others is straight forward, but kind. There is an acceptance of differences between people, and an optimism that such differences don't have to make life unpleasant.

The message is important for all of us. People <u>are</u> different, and differences can cause stress. But diversity is part of the miracle of human existence. This booklet will help people with autism, but it will also provide wisdom and optimism to everyone who shares it with a person who has autism. Read it often, and share it with others – those with autism and anyone who touches the life of someone with autism.

Roger D. Cox, Ph.D.
Director of Training
DIVISION TEACCH (Treatment and Education of Autistic and related Communication handicapped CHildren)
University of North Carolina, Chapel Hill, North Carolina, USA.

To Robert and Niall.

Thank you.

From Eileen.

Contents

Talking   **Page**   **2**

Playing   **Page**   **8**

Learning   **Page**   **20**

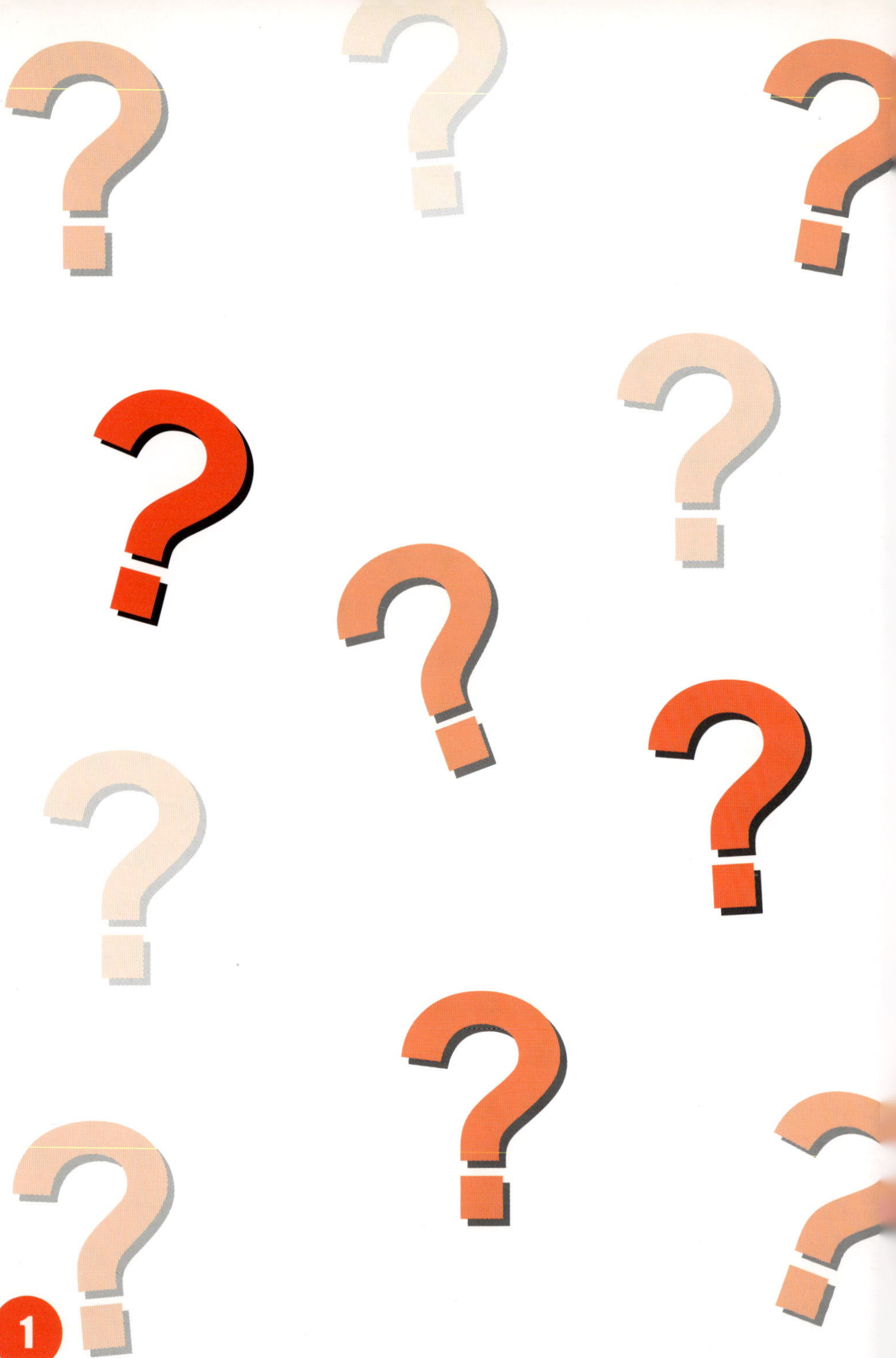

1

Talking

If you have autism you may like to talk.

You may find it difficult to think of the right words.

You may repeat words that people have said to you, just after they have spoken.

You may remember what they said and repeat the words later.

Hello, my name is Sam

My name is Sam

People who do not have autism are different from you.

They may speak in ways that seem hard to understand.

They seem to know when to take turns in their conversations.

If you have autism you may have to think very carefully about the words someone is saying to you.

You may not always understand what people mean.

It may be difficult to understand if someone is cross, or happy, or sad, or excited.

People who do not have autism are different from you.

The way someone moves their face and hands helps them understand what is being said.

They get extra meaning from the way someone's voice changes when they speak.

7

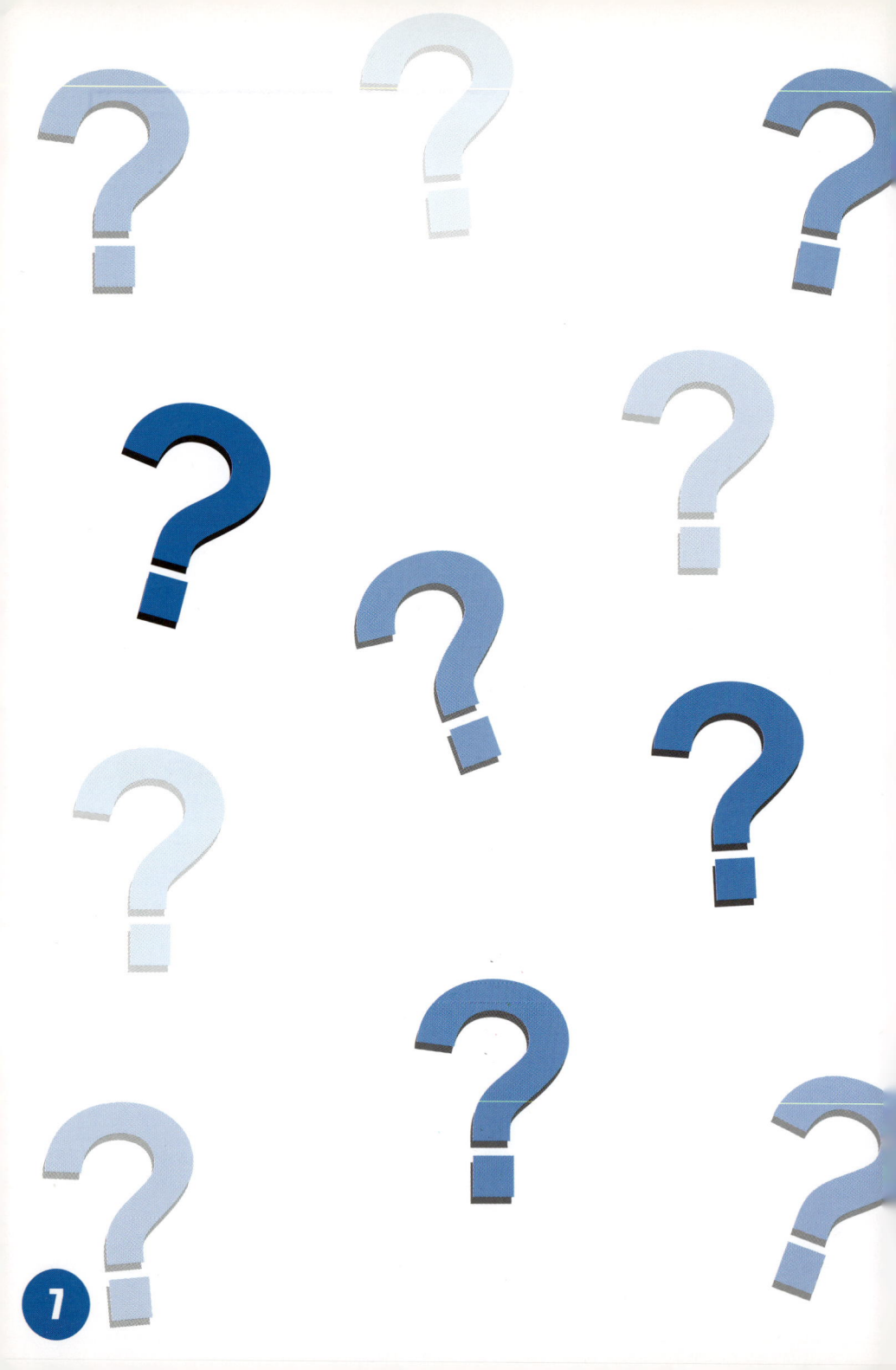

Playing

If you have autism you may prefer to play by yourself.

You may enjoy being on your own.

People who do not have autism are different from you.

They may prefer to play with other people.

They may not enjoy playing on their own for long.

If you have autism you may find it difficult being in a group with others.

You may not know when to take turns at games.

You may not understand how others are feeling.

People who do not have autism are different from you.

They may know when to take turns at games.

They may understand how another person is feeling.

They may find it hard to understand how someone who has autism is feeling.

If you have autism you may play in the same way every day.

You may like to keep your toys in special places.

It may upset you if they are moved.

You may like to spend a long time doing the same thing over and over.

Where are my videos?

People who do not have autism are different from you.

They may play with lots of different toys and games.

They like to pretend that they are other people.

They enjoy making up stories.

If you have autism you may be very tidy with your belongings.

You may like to have things in order.

You may like to put things in the right place, or in a special way.

People who do not have autism are different from you.

They can be very messy with their belongings.

They may not mind when things are put in the wrong place.

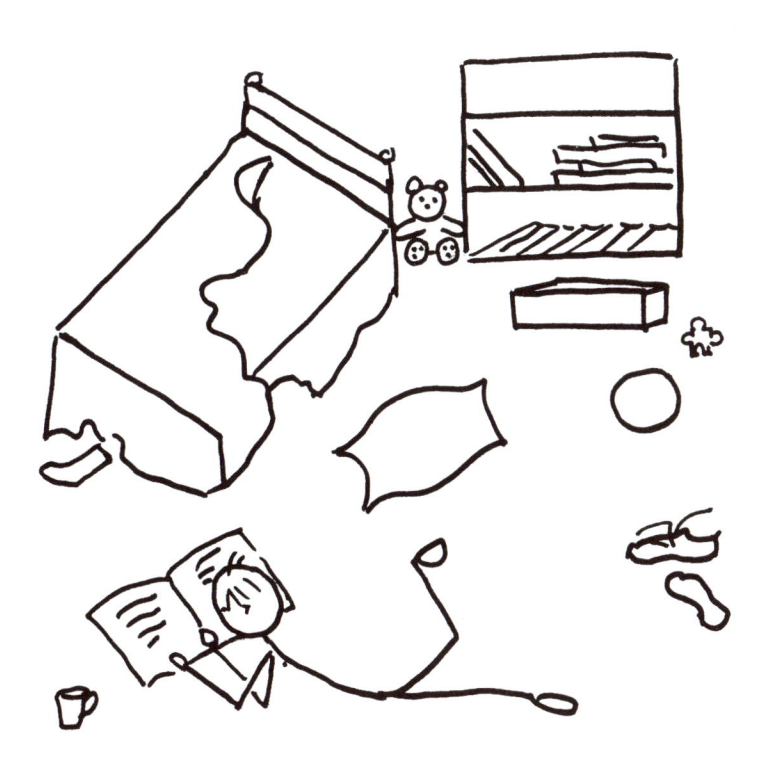

If you have autism you may be too grown up to play with toys now.

You may still like to spend time on your own.

You may put your belongings in certain places.

You may still get annoyed if things are changed.

People who do not have autism are different from you.

They may enjoy spending time with other people.

They may not mind if things are changed.

19

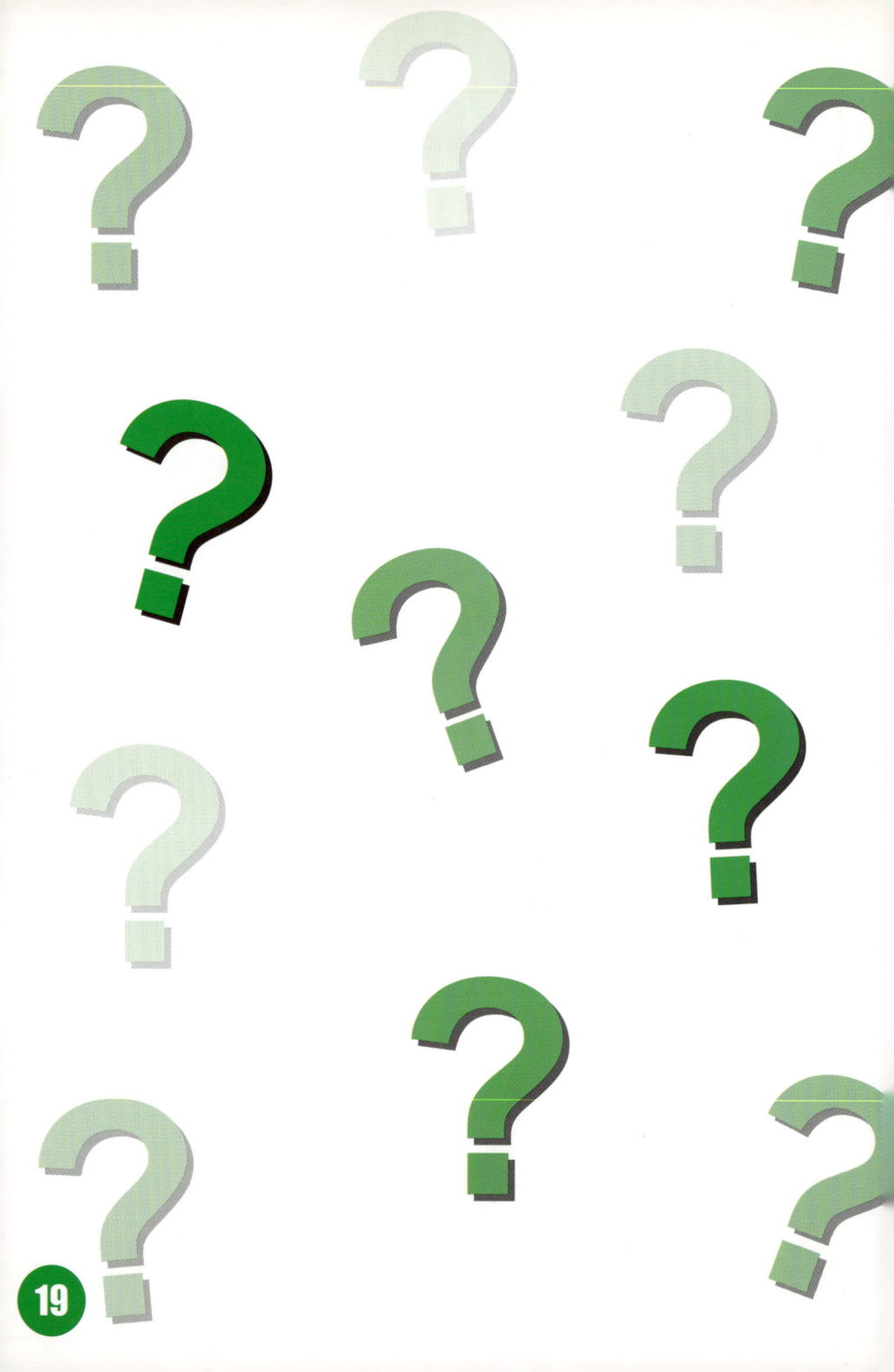

Learning

If you have autism you may find it hard to learn new things.

You may need some extra help.

You may need more time to learn new things.

Other people may be able to make things clearer for you.

People who do not have autism are different from you.

Most people find it easy to learn new things.

They may not need any extra help.

If you have autism you may find it difficult to concentrate.

You may dislike noises and interruptions when you are trying to work.

Having a special place to work can help you concentrate better on what you have to do.

You may find it hard to stop what you are doing.

People who do not have autism are different from you.

They may not mind interruptions.

They may not mind people moving about.

They can think about their work even though other people are around them.

If you have autism you may like to know when things are going to happen.

You may be upset if something changes.

It can help if you are told before it happens.

People who do not have autism are different from you.

They may not mind changes.

They sometimes enjoy when things are different.

If you have autism you may be very good at some things.

You may have a great memory.

You may be able to work some things out very quickly.

People who do not have autism are different from you.

They may find it hard to remember lots of details.

It may take them longer to do the things that you are good at.

29

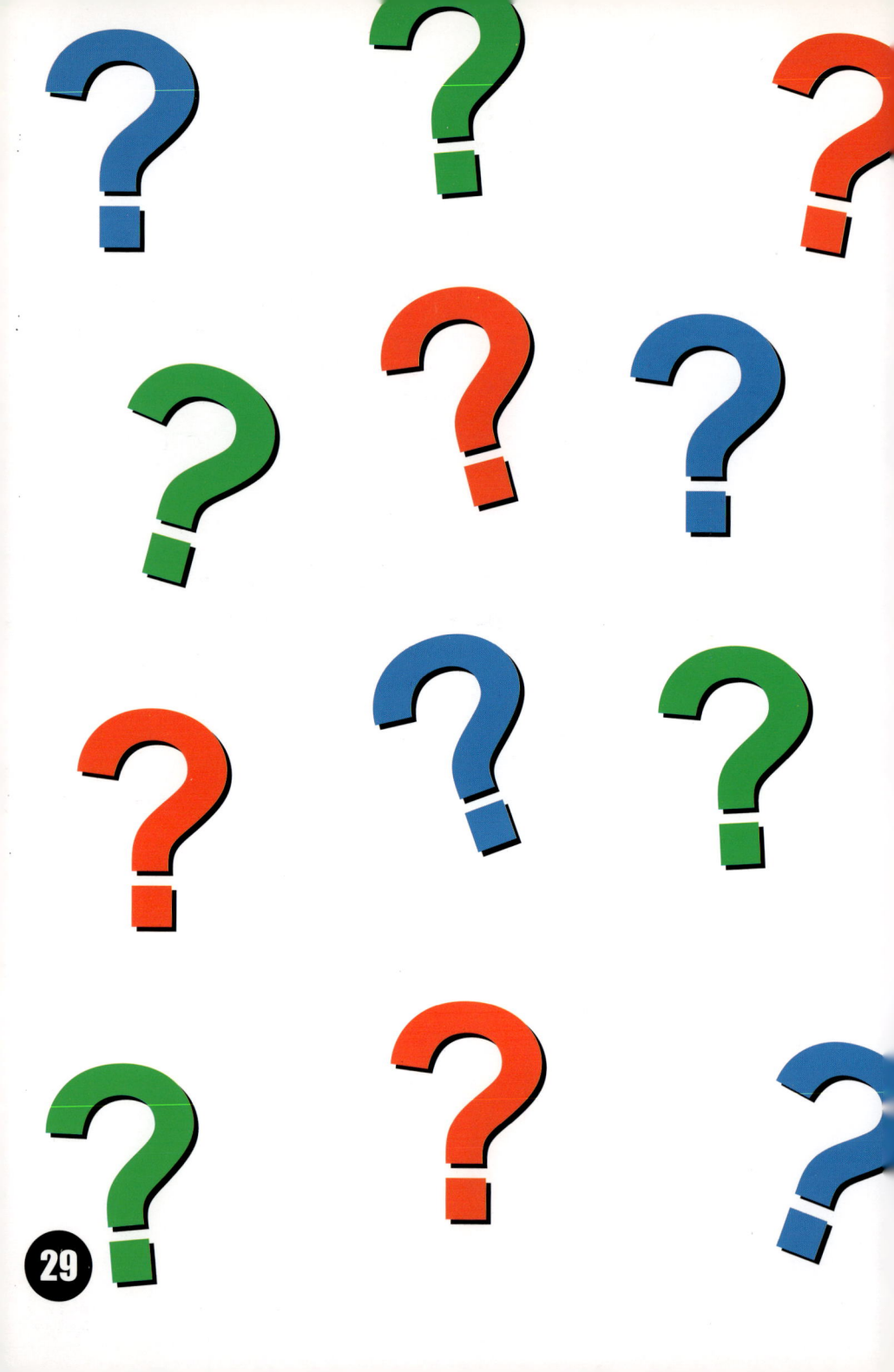

We hope you can better understand how people who do not have autism may be different from you.

We hope you can be a bit more patient with them for not understanding you and how you think about things.

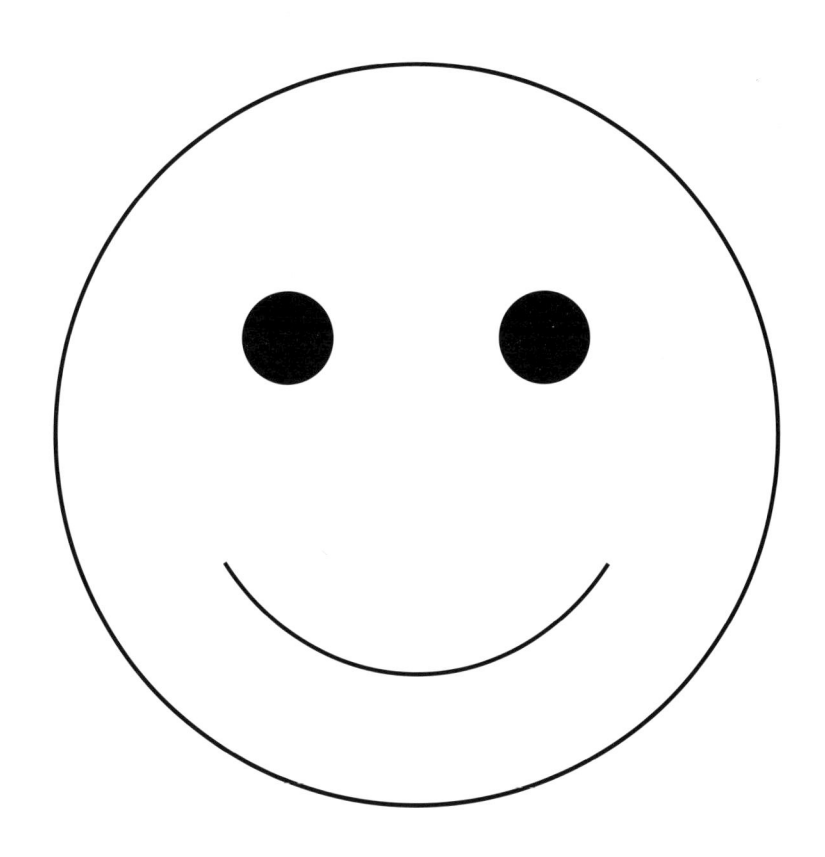

Acknowledgements

We are grateful to the Department of Health, Social Services and Public Safety for funding this publication.

Our thanks to colleagues in Division TEACCH for their support of this venture and to the charity, Parents And Professionals and Autism for help in seeking local views on the booklet. We would like to thank the many parents who shared their comments with us.

Most of all, thank you to those who are the real experts – the young people with autism who gave us their honest and important opinions.

In recognition of your help, we have included some comments that you made.